W9-AAT-792

SCHOLASTIC
News
Nonfiction Readers®

Let's Be Friends

By Amanda Miller

Children's Press®
An Imprint of Scholastic Inc.
New York Toronto London Auckland Sydney
Mexico City New Delhi Hong Kong
Danbury, Connecticut

These content vocabulary word builders are for grades 1–2.

Subject Consultant: Eli J. Lesser, MA, Director of Education, National Constitution Center, Philadelphia, Pennsylvania

Reading Consultant: Cecilia Minden-Cupp, PhD, Early Literacy Consultant and Author, Chapel Hill, North Carolina

Photographs ©2010: Alamy Images: 17 (Blend Images), 5 (Corbis UK - Fancy), 2, 19 (Kevin Dodge), 1, 12, 13 top, 13 bottom, 23 bottom (Image Source Black), 18, 22 top (Image Source Pink), cover (Photodisc); Corbis Images/Fancy/VEER: 7; IStockphoto/starfotograf: 10, 23 top; James Levin/Studio 10: 20, 21; VEER: 9 (Alloy Photography), back cover, 11 (Corbis Photography), 8, 15, 22 bottom (Digital Vision Photography).

Art Direction and Production: Scholastic Classroom Magazines

Library of Congress Cataloging-in-Publication Data

Miller, Amanda, 1974-
Let's be friends / Amanda Miller.
    p. cm. – (Scholastic news nonfiction readers)
Includes bibliographical references and index.
ISBN 13: 978-0-531-21344-5 (lib. bdg.)   978-0-531-21444-2 (pbk.)
ISBN 10: 0-531-21344-7 (lib. bdg.)   0-531-21444-3 (pbk.)
1. Friendship in children–Juvenile literature. 2. Friendship–Juvenile literature.
I. Title. II. Series.
BF723.F68M55 2009   158.2'5–dc22 2009007317

No part of this publication may be reproduced in whole or in part, or stored in a retrieval system, or transmitted in any form or by any means, electronic, mechanical, photocopying, recording, or otherwise, without written permission of the publisher. For information regarding permission, write to Scholastic Inc., 557 Broadway, New York, NY 10012.

©2010 Scholastic Inc.
All rights reserved. Published in 2010 by Children's Press, an imprint of Scholastic Inc.
Published simultaneously in Canada. Printed in China.
SCHOLASTIC, CHILDREN'S PRESS, and associated logos are trademarks and/or registered trademarks of Scholastic Inc.
1 2 3 4 5 6 7 8 9 10 R 18 17 16 15 14 13 12 11 10 09

CONTENTS

Who Are Your Friends?

Look around. Do you see your **friends**?

Friends are people you like to be with. Friends make you happy.

When was the last time you made a new friend?

friends

Your school **playground** is a good place for making friends. Ask someone new to play!

If a child asks you to play, say, "Yes." If you are already playing with friends, say, "Join us!"

You can all be friends.

You might make some new friends at the playground.

playground

What Friends Do

Friends make each other **laugh**. Anna tells Alex a funny joke. Then Alex does a funny dance.

That's what friends do!

laugh

What do you like to do with your friends?

Friends help each other.

Amy helps Jake finish the **puzzle**. Jake helps Amy reach the book on the top shelf.

That's what friends do!

puzzle

A big puzzle goes faster with a friend.

Sometimes a friend may feel sad.

When Ben is sad, Lilly wants him to feel better. Lilly tries to make him **smile**!

That's what friends do.

smile

When you are sad, it helps to have a friend.

13

Staying Friends

When friends want the same thing, they **share**.

Sometimes Grace gets the bigger piece of the last cookie. Sometimes Jen gets the bigger piece.

That's how they stay friends.

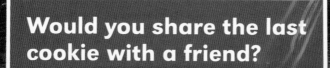

Would you share the last cookie with a friend?

Sometimes friends want to play different things. When that happens, they take turns.

First Max and James play computer games for Max. Then they play soccer for James.

That's how they stay friends.

Sometimes friends may feel **angry**. When that happens, they can talk about how they feel.

Later, they can say, "I'm sorry."

That's what friends do!

Let's be friends!

angry

LET'S PLAY TOGETHER!

American Sign Language is a way of "talking" using signs made with your hands.

Come   play

ou can use American Sign Language to ask
friend to play. Here's how:

with

me!

YOUR NEW WORDS

angry (**ang**-gree) feeling like you want to fight with someone

friends (frends) people who like being together

laugh (laf) to make a sound that shows you think something is funny

layground (**play**-ground) an outdoor area with swings, slides, or other places for children to play

uzzle (**puhz**-uhl) a game where you fit small pieces together to make one big picture

hare (shair) to divide something between two or more people

mile (smile) to turn your mouth up at the corners to show you are happy

INDEX

FIND OUT MORE
Book:
Raschka, Chris. *Yo! Yes?* New York: Scholastic, 2007.

Website:
www.tolerance.org/pt/new_friend/index_friend.html

MEET THE AUTHOR
Amanda Miller is a writer and editor for Scholastic. She and her
dog, Henry, live in Brooklyn, New York.